Mastering SEO: Your Comprehensive Guide to Boosting Online Visibility and Driving Organic Traffic

Welcome to "Mastering SEO: Your Comprehensive Guide to Boosting Online Visibility and Driving Organic Traffic." In today's digital age, having a strong online presence is essential for businesses, entrepreneurs, bloggers, and website owners. However, simply having a website or creating content is not enough. To truly succeed and stand out in the vast digital landscape, you need to harness the power of Search Engine Optimization (SEO).

SEO is the practice of optimizing your website and content to improve its visibility in search engine results. When your website ranks higher in search engines like Google, Bing, or Yahoo, you have a better chance of attracting organic traffic – visitors who find your website through their search queries. This targeted and relevant traffic can lead to increased exposure, more potential customers, and ultimately, business growth.

In this comprehensive guide, we will take you on a journey to master the art of SEO. Whether you're a beginner looking to understand the basics or an experienced marketer seeking advanced strategies, this guide will provide you with the knowledge and tools to boost your online visibility and drive organic traffic.

Throughout the chapters, we will cover various aspects of SEO, starting from the fundamentals and gradually moving into more advanced techniques. You'll learn how search engines work, why SEO is crucial for online success, and how to conduct effective keyword research to optimize your content. We'll also delve into on-page SEO, technical SEO, user experience, content optimization, link building, and analytics – all key components of a comprehensive SEO strategy.

But mastering SEO is not just about following a set of rules or applying techniques. It's about understanding the underlying principles and adapting to the ever-changing landscape of search engine algorithms. It's about creating valuable, user-friendly content that resonates with your audience and building authority and credibility in your niche.

By the end of this guide, you will have the knowledge and skills to navigate the complex world of SEO with confidence. You'll be equipped to optimize your website, create compelling content, and implement effective strategies that drive organic traffic and propel your online success.

So, whether you're a business owner seeking to grow your customer base, a blogger looking to increase your readership, or a marketer aiming to boost brand visibility, get ready to embark on a journey of mastering SEO. Let's unlock the secrets of search engine optimization and unleash the full potential of your online presence.

Understanding SEO Basics

What Is Seo?

SEO stands for Search Engine Optimization. It is the practice of optimizing a website or online content to improve its visibility and ranking on search engine results pages (SERPs). In simpler terms, SEO helps websites and online businesses to be found more easily by people searching for relevant information, products, or services on search engines like Google, Bing, or Yahoo.

The goal of SEO is to drive organic (non-paid) traffic to a website by increasing its visibility in search engine results. When a website ranks higher in search results, it is more likely to attract clicks from users, leading to increased website traffic and potential conversions.

SEO involves various strategies and techniques, including keyword research, on-page optimization, technical optimization, content creation, link building, and more. By implementing these practices, website owners can improve their website's visibility, user experience, and overall online presence.

In summary, SEO is a crucial digital marketing discipline that focuses on improving a website's search engine rankings, attracting targeted organic traffic, and ultimately increasing its visibility and online success.

Importance Of Seo In The Digital Age

In the digital age, where online presence is crucial for businesses and individuals alike, search engine optimization (SEO) has become paramount. SEO is the practice of optimizing websites and online content to improve their visibility and rankings in search engine results pages (SERPs). It is essential for several reasons:

Increased Online Visibility: With millions of websites competing for attention, SEO helps you stand out by improving your website's visibility in search engines. When your website ranks higher in SERPs, it attracts more organic traffic and exposes your brand to a wider audience.

Targeted Organic Traffic: SEO helps drive targeted organic traffic to your website. By optimizing your website for specific keywords and phrases relevant to your business, you attract visitors who are actively searching for products, services, or information related to what you offer. This targeted traffic is more likely to convert into leads or customers.

Cost-Effective Marketing: SEO is a cost-effective marketing strategy compared to traditional advertising methods. While paid advertising can deliver immediate results, it requires a continuous investment. With SEO, once you establish your online presence and improve your rankings, you can continue to attract organic traffic without ongoing ad spend.

Credibility and Trust: Higher search engine rankings contribute to building credibility and trust with your audience. When users see your website at the top of search results, they perceive it as more trustworthy and authoritative. SEO helps you establish your brand as a reliable source of information or a reputable business in your industry.

Better User Experience: SEO involves optimizing various aspects of your website, such as its structure, navigation, content, and loading speed. These optimizations enhance the user experience, making it easier for visitors to navigate your site, find relevant information, and have a seamless browsing experience. Positive user experience leads to higher engagement, lower bounce rates, and increased chances of conversions.

Competitive Advantage: In today's competitive digital landscape, SEO gives you an edge over your competitors. By consistently implementing effective SEO strategies, you can outrank your competitors in search results, attract more traffic, and gain a larger share of the market.

Long-Term Results: SEO is a long-term investment that yields sustainable results. While it may take time to see significant improvements in rankings, the efforts put into optimizing your website and content can have lasting effects. Unlike paid advertising, where visibility ends when the budget runs out, SEO continues to generate organic traffic and leads over time.

In summary, SEO is essential in the digital age to increase online visibility, drive targeted traffic, build credibility, enhance user experience, gain a competitive advantage, and achieve long-term success. By mastering SEO techniques and staying updated with the evolving search engine algorithms, you can maximize your online presence and effectively reach your target audience.

How Search Engines Work

Search engines are complex systems designed to organize and deliver relevant information to users based on their search queries. While different search engines may have slight variations in their algorithms, they generally follow a similar process to provide search results. Here's a simplified overview of how search engines work:

Crawling: Search engines use automated programs called crawlers or spiders to browse the web and discover web pages. These crawlers follow links from one page to another, collecting information about the content and structure of each page they encounter. They also update their index of web pages to ensure the most up-to-date information is available for search queries.

Indexing: Once the crawlers collect information from web pages, the search engine indexes that information. Indexing involves organizing and storing the data in a way that makes it easily accessible for search queries. The index contains various elements, including keywords, page titles, meta descriptions, and links, which help the search engine understand and retrieve relevant results.

Ranking: When a user enters a search query, the search engine uses its ranking algorithm to evaluate and prioritize the indexed pages that are most relevant to the query. The algorithm takes into account factors like keyword relevance, page quality, user experience, backlinks, and many other signals. The pages are then ranked based on their perceived relevance to the search query.

Displaying search results: The search engine presents the ranked results to the user in the form of a search engine results page (SERP). The SERP typically includes a list of web pages, each with a title, a brief description, and a URL. Users can click on the search results to visit the respective web pages for more information.

Constant updates: Search engines continuously update and refine their algorithms to deliver the most accurate and relevant search results. These updates are aimed at improving the user experience, combatting spammy or low-quality content, and adapting to changing user behavior and technology.

It's important to note that search engines strive to provide the most useful and relevant results to users, so understanding how they work can help website owners optimize their content and improve their chances of ranking higher in search results.

The Role Of Keywords In Seo

Keywords play a crucial role in SEO (Search Engine Optimization) as they are the words and phrases that users enter into search engines when looking for information, products, or services. Here's an overview of the role of keywords in SEO:

Relevance: Keywords are used to make content relevant to specific search queries. By incorporating relevant keywords into your website's content, you increase the chances of search engines recognizing your content as relevant to those keywords and displaying it in search results.

Organic Traffic: Well-optimized keywords help drive organic traffic to your website. When users search for specific keywords related to your business, and your website ranks well for those keywords, it increases the likelihood of users clicking on your website in search results and visiting your site.

Content Optimization: Keywords help guide the optimization of various elements of your website, including page titles, headings, meta descriptions, and content. By strategically incorporating keywords into these elements, search engines gain a better understanding of your content and its relevance to specific search queries.

Competitive Analysis: Keywords are also used for competitive analysis in SEO. By researching and analyzing the keywords your competitors are targeting, you can identify opportunities and develop strategies to optimize your content and outrank them in search results.

Long-Tail Keywords: Long-tail keywords, which are more specific and usually longer phrases, can be particularly valuable in SEO. While they may have lower search volume, they often have higher conversion rates as they cater to users with more specific search intent. Targeting long-tail keywords can help you attract more qualified traffic to your website.

User Intent: Understanding user intent is crucial in keyword selection. By identifying the intent behind specific keywords, you can align your content to meet those needs effectively. This ensures that your website provides relevant information and answers the questions or problems that users are searching for.

It's important to note that effective keyword usage involves a balance. Overusing keywords, known as keyword stuffing, can lead to penalties from search engines. Instead, focus on using keywords naturally and incorporating them into high-quality, valuable content that provides a great user experience. Regularly reviewing and updating your keyword strategy based on user behavior and search trends is also essential to maintain SEO effectiveness.

Importance Of User Experience And Relevance

User experience and relevance are two key factors that play a significant role in the success of SEO efforts. Here's an overview of their importance:

User Experience: Search engines, like Google, prioritize user experience in their ranking algorithms. They aim to deliver the most relevant and valuable results to users. Therefore, websites that provide a positive user experience are more likely to rank higher in search results. User experience factors include website loading speed, mobile-friendliness, ease of navigation, clear and well-organized content, and overall usability. By focusing on enhancing user experience, you not only improve your website's visibility but also increase engagement and conversion rates.

Relevance: Relevance is crucial in SEO as it determines how well your content aligns with user search queries. Search engines analyze various factors to assess the relevance of a webpage, including the use of relevant keywords, quality and depth of content, internal linking, and overall topical authority. By creating high-quality, relevant content that meets the needs and interests of your target audience, you increase your chances of ranking well in search results and attracting organic traffic that is genuinely interested in what you have to offer.

Engagement Metrics: Search engines also consider user engagement metrics, such as click-through rates (CTR), bounce rates, and time spent on page, to determine the relevance and quality of your content. If users find your website relevant and engaging, they are more likely to stay longer, explore further, and interact with your content. These positive engagement signals send a strong message to search engines that your website is valuable to users, which can lead to improved rankings.

Lower Bounce Rates: A well-optimized website with relevant and engaging content helps reduce bounce rates, which is the percentage of visitors who leave your site after viewing only one page. A high bounce rate can indicate that visitors did not find what they were looking for or that the website failed to meet their expectations. By providing a seamless and relevant user experience, you can encourage visitors to explore your website further, decreasing bounce rates and improving overall SEO performance.

Return Visits and Referrals: When users have a positive experience on your website and find your content relevant, they are more likely to return in the future and refer your website to others. This can lead to increased organic traffic, higher brand visibility, and potential backlinks from other reputable websites, all of which contribute to improved SEO rankings.

In summary, prioritizing user experience and relevance in your SEO efforts is essential for long-term success. By creating a website that offers a positive user experience, delivers relevant and valuable content, and keeps visitors engaged, you can attract organic traffic, improve search rankings, and ultimately achieve your online goals.

Conducting Effective Keyword Research

Identifying Target Keywords And Phrases

Identifying target keywords and phrases is a crucial step in SEO as it helps you optimize your content to match the search intent of your target audience. Here's a guide on how to identify target keywords and phrases:

Understand your audience: Start by gaining a clear understanding of your target audience. Who are they? What are their needs, interests, and pain points? What are they searching for when looking for products, services, or information related to your industry? This will help you align your keyword research with their search intent.

Brainstorm seed keywords: Begin by brainstorming a list of seed keywords that are relevant to your business or website. These are general terms or phrases that describe your products, services, or industry. For example, if you have an online shoe store, seed keywords could be "running shoes," "athletic footwear," or "sneakers."

Expand with keyword research tools: Utilize keyword research tools such as Google Keyword Planner, SEMrush, or Moz Keyword Explorer to expand your seed keywords into a more extensive list of potential keywords and phrases. These tools provide insights into search volume, competition, and related keywords. Look for keywords that have a good search volume and relatively low competition.

Consider long-tail keywords: Long-tail keywords are more specific and longer phrases that typically have lower search volume but higher intent. They often indicate that the searcher is looking for something more specific. For example, instead of targeting the broad keyword "running shoes," you might target a long-tail keyword like "best running shoes for flat feet." Long-tail keywords can help you reach a more targeted audience and improve your chances of ranking higher in search results.

Analyze competition: Research your competitors and see which keywords they are targeting. This can give you insights into their SEO strategies and help you identify potential keywords that you may have missed.

Consider user intent: When selecting keywords, consider the user intent behind the search. Are users looking for information, making a purchase, or seeking a specific service? Align your keywords with the intent of your target audience to ensure your content meets their needs.

Prioritize relevancy and search volume: Evaluate the relevancy and search volume of each keyword. Choose keywords that are highly relevant to your content and have a decent search volume. Aim for a balance between relevance and search volume, as targeting highly competitive keywords may be challenging for a new website.

Refine and update: Periodically review and refine your list of target keywords based on changes in the industry, search trends, and the performance of your content. Keep track of keyword rankings and make adjustments as needed.

Remember, selecting the right target keywords is an ongoing process that requires constant monitoring and adaptation. By understanding your audience, conducting thorough keyword research, and keeping up with industry trends, you can optimize your content for the most effective keywords and improve your chances of attracting organic traffic and reaching your target audience.

Tools And Techniques For Keyword Research

When it comes to keyword research, there are several tools and techniques available to help you find the most relevant and effective keywords for your SEO strategy. Here are some popular tools and techniques:

Google Keyword Planner: This free tool by Google allows you to discover keywords related to your industry or specific topics. It provides insights into search volume, competition, and keyword suggestions based on your seed keywords.

SEMrush: SEMrush is a comprehensive SEO tool that offers a wide range of features, including keyword research. It provides keyword data, search volume, competition analysis, and even allows you to explore your competitors' keyword strategies.

Moz Keyword Explorer: Moz Keyword Explorer is another powerful tool that helps you find and prioritize keywords. It provides valuable data on search volume, keyword difficulty, organic click-through rate, and other metrics to assist you in choosing the right keywords for your content.

Long-tail keyword research: Long-tail keywords are specific, longer phrases that target a more niche audience. Tools like Answer the Public, Keywordtool.io, and Ubersuggest can help you identify long-tail keyword variations and related search queries based on your seed keywords.

Competitor analysis: Analyzing your competitors' websites and content can give you insights into the keywords they are targeting. Tools like SEMrush and Ahrefs allow you to enter a competitor's domain and view the keywords they are ranking for, helping you discover new keyword opportunities.

Google Trends: Google Trends allows you to explore the popularity of specific keywords over time. It provides insights into seasonal trends, geographic data, and related queries, helping you identify trending keywords and topics.

Social media platforms: Monitoring social media platforms like Twitter, Facebook, and Instagram can give you insights into trending topics and popular keywords within your industry. Look for hashtags and keywords that are frequently used by your target audience.

Customer surveys and feedback: Engaging with your audience through surveys, feedback forms, or social media conversations can provide valuable insights into the language they use and the specific terms they associate with your products or services. This can help you uncover relevant keywords that resonate with your target audience.

Remember, keyword research is an ongoing process, and it's essential to regularly review and update your keyword strategy based on changes in the industry, search trends, and the performance of your content. By utilizing these tools and techniques, you can uncover high-performing keywords that will drive organic traffic to your website and improve your overall SEO efforts.

Analyzing Keyword Competition And Search Volume

Analyzing keyword competition and search volume is crucial in determining the viability and potential impact of specific keywords for your SEO strategy. Here's how you can approach these factors:

Keyword Competition:

- Search Engine Results Pages (SERPs): Conduct a manual search on search engines like Google using your target keyword. Evaluate the top-ranking pages and assess their quality, relevance, and authority. If the top results are dominated by authoritative and well-established websites, it indicates high competition.

- SEO Tools: Utilize SEO tools like SEMrush, Moz, or Ahrefs to analyze keyword difficulty scores. These tools provide insights into the competitiveness of keywords by considering factors such as domain authority, backlink profiles, and content quality of the top-ranking pages.
- Long-tail Keywords: Long-tail keywords often have lower competition as they are more specific. Targeting long-tail keywords can be advantageous, especially if your website or content is relatively new or has lower domain authority.

Search Volume:

- Keyword Research Tools: Tools like Google Keyword Planner, SEMrush, or Moz provide search volume data for keywords. This data represents the average monthly search volume for a given keyword, giving you an indication of its popularity and potential traffic.
- Trend Analysis: Use Google Trends or other trend analysis tools to assess the search volume patterns of specific keywords over time. This helps identify seasonal variations and emerging trends that may impact keyword search volume.
- Target Audience: Consider the relevance of the keyword to your target audience. High search volume may not always align with your target market if the keyword is too broad or not specific enough. Focus on keywords that align with your audience's needs and intent.

It's important to strike a balance between competition and search volume when selecting keywords. Highly competitive keywords may be challenging to rank for, especially for new websites, while low-competition keywords with very low search volume may not generate significant traffic. Aim for keywords that have a reasonable search volume and a manageable level of competition, allowing you to rank well and attract relevant traffic to your website.

Regularly monitoring and adjusting your keyword strategy based on changes in competition and search volume will help optimize your SEO efforts and ensure your content aligns with user intent and current market trends.

On-Page SEO Optimization

Optimizing Website Structure And Navigation

Optimizing website structure and navigation is an essential aspect of SEO. A well-structured and user-friendly website not only improves the user experience but also helps search engines understand your content better. Here are some tips to optimize your website structure and navigation:

Logical Hierarchy: Organize your website content in a logical hierarchy, with a clear and intuitive structure. Use a top-down approach, starting with broader categories (e.g., main navigation menu) and progressively drilling down into subcategories and individual pages. This hierarchy helps both users and search engines navigate and understand your website's content.

Clear URL Structure: Ensure your URLs are descriptive and reflect the content of the page. Use keywords when appropriate to provide context to both users and search engines. A clear URL structure makes it easier for search engines to crawl and index your website.

Intuitive Navigation Menu: Design a user-friendly navigation menu that is easy to understand and navigate. Use clear and concise labels for menu items, and consider dropdown menus or submenus for organizing subcategories. Include a search bar to facilitate quick content discovery.

Internal Linking: Implement a strategic internal linking strategy throughout your website. Internal links help search engines discover and navigate your content, while also spreading link equity throughout your website. Link related pages together using anchor text that includes relevant keywords.

Mobile-Friendly Design: With the increasing use of mobile devices, it's crucial to have a responsive website design that adapts to different screen sizes. Ensure your website is mobile-friendly and provides a seamless user experience across all devices.

XML Sitemap: Create an XML sitemap and submit it to search engines like Google. A sitemap helps search engines understand the structure of your website and ensures all pages are crawled and indexed.

User Experience (UX): Pay attention to the overall user experience of your website. Ensure fast page load times, easy navigation, and clear calls-to-action. User-friendly websites tend to have lower bounce rates and higher engagement, which can positively impact your SEO.

Site Architecture: Consider the overall architecture of your website, especially if you have a large website with multiple sections or subdomains. Determine the most logical and efficient way to organize and connect different parts of your website to provide a seamless user experience.

By optimizing your website structure and navigation, you create a well-organized and user-friendly website that is not only attractive to visitors but also search engine friendly. This improves your chances of ranking higher in search engine results, attracting more organic traffic, and enhancing the overall success of your SEO efforts.

Creating Compelling Meta Titles And Descriptions

Creating compelling meta titles and descriptions is an important aspect of on-page SEO. Meta titles and descriptions are HTML elements that provide concise summaries of your web page content in search engine results. Here are some tips for creating compelling meta titles and descriptions:

Keyword Relevance: Include relevant keywords in your meta title and description to signal to search engines and users what your page is about. This helps improve your visibility in search results and attracts relevant traffic.

Unique and Descriptive: Make sure each meta title and description is unique for every page on your website. Use descriptive language that accurately reflects the content of the page. This helps users understand what they can expect when they click on your link.

Compelling and Engaging: Write meta titles and descriptions that are compelling and encourage users to click through to your website. Use persuasive language, a clear call-to-action, and highlight unique selling points or benefits of your content.

Length Guidelines: Keep your meta titles under 60 characters and meta descriptions under 160 characters to ensure they are fully displayed in search engine results. If they are too long, they may get truncated, potentially affecting the user's understanding and click-through decision.

Use Power Words: Incorporate power words or action verbs that evoke emotion and create a sense of urgency. This can help capture the attention of users and increase click-through rates.

Maintain Relevance: Ensure that your meta titles and descriptions accurately reflect the content of your page. Misleading or irrelevant meta information may lead to higher bounce rates and negatively impact user experience.

Test and Optimize: Regularly monitor the performance of your meta titles and descriptions using tools like Google Analytics or Search Console. Analyze click-through rates and make adjustments to improve their effectiveness over time.

Consider Branding: If applicable, include your brand name or website name in the meta title or description. This helps users recognize your brand in search results and builds brand visibility and trust.

Remember that meta titles and descriptions are not direct ranking factors for search engines. However, they play a crucial role in attracting users' attention and encouraging them to click on your link. By creating compelling, relevant, and optimized meta titles and descriptions, you can improve your click-through rates, drive more organic traffic to your website, and enhance your overall SEO efforts.

Incorporating Keywords In Headings, Content, And Urls

Incorporating keywords strategically in headings, content, and URLs is an essential aspect of on-page SEO. It helps search engines understand the relevance and topic of your web page and improves your chances of ranking for relevant search queries. Here's how you can optimize these elements:

Headings (H1, H2, etc.): Use heading tags (H1, H2, H3, etc.) to structure your content and indicate the hierarchy of information. Incorporate your target keywords naturally in the headings while ensuring they accurately reflect the content of the section. This helps search engines and users quickly grasp the main topics covered on your page.

Content: Create high-quality, informative, and engaging content that provides value to your audience. Incorporate your target keywords throughout the content, but ensure it reads naturally and is not overly stuffed with keywords. Use variations of the keywords, synonyms, and related terms to make the content more comprehensive and relevant.

URLs: Optimize your URLs to include relevant keywords that reflect the content of the page. Keep them concise, descriptive, and user-friendly. Avoid using generic or random alphanumeric strings. Instead, include the primary keyword or key phrase, separating words with hyphens for readability.

Image Alt Text: When using images on your website, include descriptive and keyword-rich alt text. Alt text helps search engines understand the content of the image and can also appear as text when an image fails to load. This provides an opportunity to incorporate relevant keywords and improve accessibility.

Internal Linking: Use internal links within your content to connect related pages on your website. When linking, use descriptive anchor text that includes relevant keywords. This helps search engines understand the context and relationship between different pages on your site.

Keyword Density: While it's important to include keywords in your content, avoid keyword stuffing. Maintain a natural keyword density and focus on creating valuable and user-friendly content. Keyword density guidelines can vary, but a general rule of thumb is to keep it below 2-3% to avoid keyword over-optimization.

User Experience: Ensure that your content is well-structured, easy to read, and provides a positive user experience. Use headings to break up the text, incorporate bullet points or numbered lists for clarity, and write in a way that engages and satisfies your audience. User-friendly content is more likely to be shared and linked to, further enhancing your SEO efforts.

Remember, the key is to strike a balance between optimizing for search engines and providing a valuable user experience. By incorporating keywords naturally and strategically in headings, content, and URLs, you can improve the relevance and visibility of your web pages, ultimately driving organic traffic and improving your search engine rankings.

Utilizing Image Alt Tags And Optimizing Multimedia Elements

Incorporating image alt tags and optimizing multimedia elements is an important aspect of on-page SEO. Here's how you can make the most of these elements to improve your website's visibility:

Image Alt Tags: Alt tags, also known as alt attributes or alt text, are descriptions of images that appear in place of the image when it fails to load or for visually impaired users who rely on screen readers. Alt tags serve two purposes: improving accessibility and providing search engines with information about the image.

Use descriptive alt tags: Write concise and accurate descriptions that convey the content and context of the image. Incorporate relevant keywords naturally, but avoid keyword stuffing. Be specific and provide meaningful information to enhance both user experience and SEO.

Image File Names: When naming your image files, use descriptive and keyword-rich filenames. Instead of generic names like "image001.jpg," rename the file to reflect the image's content and include relevant keywords. For example, "blue-widget.jpg" is more informative and SEO-friendly.

Image Size and Compression: Optimize your images for web by resizing them to the appropriate dimensions and compressing them without sacrificing quality. Large image file sizes can slow down your website, affecting user experience and search engine rankings. Use image optimization tools or plugins to reduce file sizes while maintaining visual clarity.

Video Optimization: If you have videos on your website, optimize them for search engines. Provide keyword-rich titles, descriptions, and tags for your videos. Host videos on reputable platforms like YouTube or Vimeo and embed them on your website, as search engines can index and rank videos from these platforms.

Captions and Transcripts: If you include videos or audio content, consider adding captions or transcripts. Captions not only make your multimedia accessible to a wider audience, including those with hearing impairments, but they also provide textual content that search engines can crawl and index, improving your SEO.

Schema Markup: Use schema markup to provide additional structured data about your multimedia elements. Schema markup helps search engines understand the content and context of your images, videos, and other media. It can enhance search engine visibility and improve the chances of rich media snippets appearing in search results.

Mobile Optimization: Ensure that your multimedia elements are mobile-friendly and responsive. With the increasing use of mobile devices for browsing, it's crucial to optimize your images and videos for different screen sizes and ensure they load quickly on mobile devices.

By optimizing image alt tags, filenames, multimedia elements, and incorporating relevant schema markup, you can enhance the visibility and accessibility of your website's visual content. This, in turn, improves your chances of ranking higher in search engine results, attracting organic traffic, and providing a better user experience.

Technical SEO Essentials

Website Speed And Performance Optimization

Website speed and performance optimization is crucial for SEO and user experience. A slow-loading website can lead to higher bounce rates, lower search engine rankings, and a negative impact on conversions. Here are some strategies to optimize your website's speed and performance:

Minimize HTTP Requests: Reduce the number of HTTP requests by combining or minifying CSS and JavaScript files. This reduces the overall file size and improves loading speed.

Enable Browser Caching: Set up caching headers to instruct browsers to store static resources like images, CSS, and JavaScript files. This way, returning visitors don't need to re-download the same files, resulting in faster load times.

Compress and Optimize Images: Resize and compress images to reduce their file size without compromising quality. Use image optimization tools or plugins to automatically compress images and serve them in the appropriate format.

Enable GZIP Compression: Enable GZIP compression on your server to compress website files before sending them to the browser. This significantly reduces file sizes and speeds up page load times.

Minify CSS and JavaScript: Minify your CSS and JavaScript files by removing unnecessary whitespace, comments, and code formatting. This reduces file sizes and improves loading speed.

Use a Content Delivery Network (CDN): A CDN stores your

website's static files on servers distributed worldwide. When a user visits your site, the files are served from the nearest server, reducing latency and improving loading times.

Optimize Database and Code: Regularly optimize your website's database by removing unnecessary data, optimizing queries, and cleaning up your code. This helps improve the overall performance of your website.

Implement Caching: Utilize caching mechanisms like page caching, object caching, and database caching to store dynamically generated content and reduce server load. This allows your website to serve cached content instead of generating it from scratch with each request.

Monitor and Remove Unused Plugins: Regularly review your website's plugins and remove any that are no longer necessary. Unused plugins can slow down your site and increase the risk of security vulnerabilities.

Test and Monitor Website Speed: Regularly test your website's speed using tools like Google PageSpeed Insights, GTmetrix, or Pingdom. Monitor your website's performance to identify areas for improvement and make necessary optimizations.

Remember, a fast and responsive website not only improves user experience but also sends positive signals to search engines, potentially boosting your search rankings. By implementing these website speed and performance optimization strategies, you can create a smooth and efficient browsing experience for your visitors while maximizing your chances of online success.

Mobile-Friendliness And Responsive Design

In today's digital landscape, mobile devices play a significant role in online browsing and search. Ensuring your website is mobile-friendly and incorporates responsive design is crucial for SEO and user experience. Here's why:

User Preference: With the increasing use of smartphones and tablets, users expect websites to be optimized for mobile devices. If your site is not mobile-friendly, visitors may have difficulty navigating and accessing content, leading to frustration and a higher bounce rate.

Search Engine Rankings: Google prioritizes mobile-friendly websites in its search results, especially for mobile searches. Having a mobile-friendly website gives you a competitive advantage and improves your chances of ranking higher in mobile search results.

User Experience: Responsive design ensures that your website adapts to different screen sizes and devices, providing an optimal viewing and browsing experience. Content, images, and menus adjust automatically, making it easier for users to navigate and engage with your site.

Decreased Bounce Rate: A mobile-friendly website enhances user engagement and reduces bounce rates. When users have a positive experience on your site, they are more likely to stay longer, explore further, and potentially convert into customers or subscribers.

Improved Loading Speed: Mobile-friendly websites are optimized for faster loading on mobile devices. Mobile users expect quick access to information, and a slow-loading site can lead to frustration and abandonment. By implementing responsive design, you can optimize your site's loading speed for mobile users.

Social Sharing and Link Building: Mobile-friendly websites are more likely to be shared on social media platforms and linked to by other websites. This can increase your online visibility, drive traffic, and improve your overall SEO efforts.

To ensure mobile-friendliness and responsive design:

Use a Responsive Website Theme or Template: Choose a responsive website theme or template that automatically adjusts your site's layout and elements based on the device being used.

Optimize Images and Media: Compress and optimize images and media files to reduce file sizes and improve loading speed on mobile devices.

Test Across Multiple Devices: Test your website across various mobile devices, including smartphones and tablets, to ensure consistent functionality and usability.

Simplify Navigation: Simplify your website's navigation for mobile users by using clear menus, dropdowns, and easy-to-tap buttons.

Prioritize Content Placement: Place your most important content and call-to-action elements prominently on the mobile version of your site to capture the attention of mobile users quickly.

Use Mobile-Friendly Forms: If your website includes forms, make sure they are mobile-friendly with easily tappable fields and properly sized input areas.

Remember, catering to the mobile audience is essential for a successful online presence. By embracing mobile-friendliness and responsive design, you create a seamless and enjoyable experience for mobile users, improve your search engine rankings, and increase your chances of attracting and retaining visitors.

Website Indexing And Xml Sitemaps

Website indexing and XML sitemaps play a crucial role in SEO by helping search engines understand and navigate your website's structure and content. Here's what you need to know:

Website Indexing: Search engines use web crawlers (also known as spiders or bots) to scan and index web pages. Indexing involves the process of collecting and storing information about your website's pages, including their URLs, content, meta tags, and other relevant data. This enables search engines to retrieve and display relevant results when users perform searches.

XML Sitemaps: An XML sitemap is a file that lists all the pages on your website, along with additional information such as the last modification date, priority, and frequency of updates. XML sitemaps serve as a roadmap for search engine crawlers, guiding them to discover and index your web pages more efficiently.

Benefits of XML Sitemaps: XML sitemaps offer several benefits for SEO:

- Improved Crawling: By providing a clear and comprehensive list of your website's pages, XML sitemaps help search engines discover and crawl your content more effectively. This is especially useful for large websites, new websites with limited external links, or websites with complex navigation.
- Indexing of Deeply Nested Pages: XML sitemaps ensure that search engines can find and index all the pages on your website, even those buried deep within the site's structure. This is particularly important for pages that might not be easily accessible through internal links.
- Priority and Frequency Indication: XML sitemaps allow you to specify the priority and frequency of updates for each page. This provides search engines with valuable information about the importance and freshness of

your content.

- Enhanced SEO Performance: By ensuring that all your pages are indexed and properly considered for search engine rankings, XML sitemaps can improve your overall SEO performance and increase the visibility of your website in search results.

Creating an XML Sitemap: You can generate an XML sitemap using various tools and plugins, or you can create it manually. Ensure that your XML sitemap is accurate, up to date, and follows the XML sitemap protocol. Once created, submit your XML sitemap to search engines through their webmaster tools or search console.

Regular Updates: As you add new pages, make changes to existing ones, or remove outdated content, update your XML sitemap accordingly. This ensures that search engines have the latest information about your website's structure and content.

Monitoring and Troubleshooting: Regularly monitor your website's indexing status and use webmaster tools to identify any issues or errors related to indexing and XML sitemaps. This helps you identify potential crawl errors, missing pages, or other problems that may affect your website's visibility in search results.

Remember, a well-optimized XML sitemap enhances your website's crawlability, ensures comprehensive indexing, and improves your chances of ranking higher in search engine results. By implementing and maintaining an XML sitemap, you provide search engines with a clear understanding of your website's structure and content, ultimately boosting your SEO efforts.

Handling Duplicate Content And Url Canonicalization

Handling duplicate content and URL canonicalization are important aspects of SEO to ensure that search engines properly index and rank your website. Here's what you need to know:

Duplicate Content: Duplicate content refers to identical or very similar content that appears on multiple web pages, either within your own website or across different websites. Duplicate content can confuse search engines and dilute the ranking potential of your pages. It's important to address duplicate content issues to maintain a strong SEO presence.

Causes of Duplicate Content: Duplicate content can occur due to various reasons, such as:

- Multiple URLs for the same content: If your website allows different URLs to access the same content (e.g., through different parameters, session IDs, or tracking codes), it can lead to duplicate content issues.
- WWW vs. non-WWW versions: Having both www and non-www versions of your website can create duplicate content problems. Search engines may view these as separate entities and index them separately.
- HTTP vs. HTTPS: Similarly, having both HTTP and HTTPS versions of your website can cause duplicate content issues.
- Content syndication: If your content is syndicated or published on other websites without proper attribution or canonical tags, it can result in duplicate content.

URL Canonicalization: URL canonicalization is the process of selecting the preferred URL when multiple URLs can access the same content. It helps search engines understand the canonical or primary version of the page to index and rank.

Resolving Duplicate Content Issues:

- Set a preferred domain: Choose whether you want your website to be accessed with or without the "www" prefix and ensure consistent internal linking and redirects to the preferred version.
- Implement 301 redirects: If you have multiple versions of the same content or URLs, use 301 redirects to redirect users and search engines to the preferred URL. This consolidates the ranking signals and prevents indexing of duplicate pages.
- Use canonical tags: If you have similar content on different pages, use canonical tags to indicate the preferred version. The canonical tag specifies the canonical URL that search engines should consider for indexing and ranking.
- Avoid content scraping: Monitor your content and take action against websites that scrape or duplicate your content without permission. Reach out to those websites and request proper attribution or removal of the duplicated content.
- Syndication with proper attribution: If you syndicate your content, ensure that the syndicating websites provide proper attribution and include canonical tags pointing back to the original source.
- Consistent internal linking: Ensure that your internal links point to the preferred URL version to consolidate ranking signals and avoid confusion.

Regular Monitoring: Regularly monitor your website for duplicate content using tools like Google Search Console or third-party SEO tools. These tools can help you identify duplicate content issues and take corrective actions promptly.

By addressing duplicate content and implementing proper URL canonicalization, you ensure that search engines understand the correct version of your content and can effectively index and rank your web pages. This helps improve your SEO performance and prevents dilution of ranking signals caused by duplicate content.

User Experience and Content Optimization

Importance Of User-Friendly Website Design

User-friendly website design plays a crucial role in the success of your website and its overall user experience. Here are some key reasons why it is important:

Enhanced User Experience: User-friendly design ensures that visitors can easily navigate and interact with your website. It focuses on providing a seamless and intuitive experience, making it easier for users to find the information they need, engage with your content, and perform desired actions. This leads to higher user satisfaction and encourages them to stay longer on your site, explore more pages, and potentially convert into customers or subscribers.

Improved Usability: User-friendly design takes into consideration the usability principles, such as clear navigation, logical layout, readable typography, and intuitive interface elements. By making your website easy to use and understand, you reduce friction and frustration for your visitors. They can quickly locate the desired information, access important features, and complete tasks efficiently. This leads to a positive user experience and encourages repeat visits.

Increased Engagement and Conversions: A user-friendly website design encourages visitors to engage with your content and take desired actions, such as filling out a form, making a purchase, or subscribing to a newsletter. By removing barriers and providing a smooth user experience, you can increase the likelihood of conversions. Intuitive forms, prominent calls-to-action, and streamlined checkout processes are some examples of user-friendly design elements that can boost conversion rates.

Mobile Responsiveness: With the increasing use of mobile devices, having a user-friendly and mobile-responsive website is essential. Mobile-responsive design ensures that your website adapts to different screen sizes and resolutions, providing an optimal viewing experience on smartphones and tablets. This not only caters to the growing mobile user base but also improves your website's visibility in search engine results, as mobile-friendliness is a ranking factor for search engines like Google.

Positive Brand Perception: A well-designed and user-friendly website reflects positively on your brand. It demonstrates professionalism, attention to detail, and a commitment to delivering a great user experience. Visitors are more likely to trust and engage with a website that is visually appealing, easy to navigate, and provides value through its content and functionality. A positive brand perception can lead to increased credibility, customer loyalty, and word-of-mouth referrals.

SEO Benefits: User-friendly design indirectly contributes to your website's search engine optimization (SEO). Search engines consider user experience signals, such as bounce rate, time on site, and engagement metrics, when determining search rankings. If visitors have a positive experience on your site and stay longer, it sends a signal to search engines that your website is valuable and relevant, potentially boosting its visibility in search results.

In summary, a user-friendly website design is vital for providing a positive user experience, improving usability, increasing engagement and conversions, catering to mobile users, enhancing brand perception, and supporting your SEO efforts. By prioritizing user needs and designing with usability in mind, you can create a website that delights visitors, drives results, and sets your business apart from the competition.

Creating High-Quality, Engaging Content

Creating high-quality and engaging content is a key aspect of any successful website or online presence. Here are some strategies to help you produce compelling content:

Know Your Audience: Understand your target audience's needs, preferences, and interests. Conduct thorough research to identify the topics, language, and tone that resonate with them. Tailor your content to address their pain points, answer their questions, and provide value.

Provide Valuable Information: Offer informative and insightful content that educates, entertains, or solves a problem for your audience. Share your expertise, industry knowledge, and unique perspectives to establish yourself as a trusted authority. Use credible sources and data to support your claims and provide evidence.

Use Engaging Formats: Experiment with various content formats to keep your audience engaged. This can include blog posts, articles, videos, infographics, podcasts, and interactive elements like quizzes or surveys. Mix up your content to cater to different learning preferences and capture attention.

Craft Compelling Headlines: Create attention-grabbing headlines that pique curiosity and encourage readers to click and explore further. A well-crafted headline should be concise, descriptive, and convey the value or benefit of reading the content. Use power words, numbers, or thought-provoking statements to make your headline stand out.

Write Clear and Concise Copy: Make your content easy to read and understand. Use clear and concise language, break up long paragraphs, and use headings, subheadings, and bullet points to enhance readability. Use a conversational tone to connect with your audience and avoid jargon or overly technical terms unless necessary.

Incorporate Visual Elements: Include relevant and eye-catching visuals, such as images, charts, or infographics, to enhance your content's appeal and convey information in a visually appealing way. Visuals can break up text, make complex concepts easier to understand, and increase engagement.

Tell Stories: Humans are naturally drawn to stories. Incorporate storytelling techniques into your content to make it more relatable and emotionally resonant. Use anecdotes, case studies, or personal experiences to illustrate your points and connect with your audience on a deeper level.

Encourage Interaction and Discussion: Foster engagement by inviting readers to leave comments, share their opinions, or ask questions at the end of your content. Respond to comments and encourage conversation to create a sense of community around your content.

Optimize for SEO: Ensure your content is optimized for search engines by incorporating relevant keywords, meta tags, and descriptive URLs. Conduct keyword research to identify popular search terms related to your topic and strategically include them in your content without compromising readability.

Edit and Proofread: Before publishing your content, carefully review and edit for clarity, grammar, spelling, and overall quality. Typos and errors can detract from your credibility and professionalism. Consider having someone else review your content to catch any mistakes or provide feedback.

Remember, consistently producing high-quality and engaging content is key to attracting and retaining your audience. Strive to deliver value, provide an enjoyable reading experience, and address the needs and interests of your target audience. By doing so, you can establish yourself as a trusted resource and drive ongoing traffic and engagement to your website.

Optimizing Content Readability And Formatting

Optimizing content readability and formatting is crucial to keep your audience engaged and ensure they can easily consume your content. Here are some tips to enhance readability and formatting:

Use Clear and Concise Language: Write in a way that is easy to understand. Use simple language, avoid jargon, and explain complex concepts in a clear and concise manner. Break down information into smaller, digestible chunks to make it more reader-friendly.

Organize Content with Headings and Subheadings: Structure your content using headings and subheadings to create a logical flow and guide readers through your article. Headings also make it easier for readers to skim and find the information they need. Use descriptive and keyword-rich headings to improve SEO.

Break up Text with Paragraphs and Bullets: Avoid long paragraphs that can overwhelm readers. Instead, use shorter paragraphs to make your content more scannable and readable. Additionally, use bulleted or numbered lists to present information in a concise and organized manner.

Utilize White Space: White space, or empty space between paragraphs and sections, improves readability and gives your content a clean and visually appealing look. It allows readers to focus on the text without feeling overwhelmed by a cluttered layout.

Incorporate Visual Elements: Use images, infographics, and other visual elements to break up text and add visual interest to your content. Visuals not only make your content more appealing but also help in conveying information more effectively.

Emphasize Key Points: Highlight important information by using bold or italicized text. This helps readers quickly identify the main takeaways or key points of your content. However, use emphasis sparingly to avoid overwhelming the reader or diluting the impact.

Use Appropriate Font and Font Size: Choose a font that is easy to read on different devices and screen sizes. Stick to standard web-safe fonts to ensure compatibility. Additionally, use an appropriate font size that is comfortable for reading both on desktop and mobile devices.

Incorporate Multimedia: Consider including multimedia elements like videos or audio clips to enhance the content experience. This can help engage readers and provide a more interactive and dynamic experience.

Proofread and Edit: Errors and typos can negatively impact the readability of your content. Always proofread and edit your content before publishing. Check for spelling and grammar mistakes, and ensure that your sentences flow smoothly.

Test Readability: Consider using readability tools or plugins to analyze the readability of your content. These tools provide insights into factors like sentence length, word complexity, and overall readability score. Aim for a readability level that matches your target audience's comprehension abilities.

By optimizing content readability and formatting, you create a more enjoyable and accessible reading experience for your audience. This, in turn, encourages them to stay longer on your page, engage with your content, and increases the chances of them returning for more.

Incorporating Multimedia Elements Effectively

Incorporating multimedia elements can greatly enhance your content and engage your audience. Here are some tips for incorporating multimedia effectively:

Choose Relevant and High-Quality Media: Select multimedia elements that are directly related to your content and support your message. Whether it's images, videos, infographics, or audio clips, ensure they are of high quality and align with the overall theme and tone of your content.

Use Visuals to Complement Text: Visuals can help break up text-heavy content and make it more visually appealing. Use images or infographics to illustrate key points, provide examples, or enhance understanding. Visuals should support and reinforce your written content rather than distract from it.

Optimize Image Size and Format: Ensure that your images are properly optimized for web viewing to avoid slow loading times. Compress the image files to reduce their size without compromising quality. Use appropriate file formats such as JPEG or PNG, depending on the type of image and its purpose.

Add Captions and Descriptions: When including images or videos, provide captions or descriptions to give context and improve accessibility. Captions can also help reinforce your message and draw the reader's attention to important details.

Embed Videos: If you include videos, consider embedding them directly into your content. This allows readers to view the video without leaving the page, providing a seamless and immersive experience. Make sure the video player is responsive and compatible with different devices.

Use Audio for Additional Engagement: Audio elements, such as podcasts or sound clips, can be a powerful way to engage your audience. They provide an alternative way of consuming content and cater to different learning preferences. Make sure to include a play button or audio controls for easy playback.

Balance Multimedia with Text: While multimedia elements are valuable, it's important to strike a balance and not overwhelm your content with too many visuals or videos. Ensure that the multimedia supports and enhances the text rather than overshadowing it. Use them strategically to convey information effectively.

Test Compatibility and Responsiveness: Ensure that your multimedia elements are compatible with different devices and screen sizes. Test your content on various devices, such as desktops, smartphones, and tablets, to ensure a seamless viewing experience for all users.

Consider Accessibility: Make your multimedia elements accessible to users with disabilities. Provide alternative text for images, captions for videos, and transcripts for audio content. This ensures that all users can engage with and understand your multimedia elements.

Regularly Update and Maintain Multimedia: Keep your multimedia elements up to date by periodically reviewing and replacing outdated or irrelevant content. Broken links or non-functional media can negatively impact user experience, so regularly check and update your multimedia elements.

By incorporating multimedia elements effectively, you can enhance the visual appeal, engagement, and overall impact of your content. Remember to choose multimedia that aligns with your message, supports your content, and provides value to your audience.

Link Building and Off-Page SEO

Understanding The Role Of Backlinks In Seo

Backlinks play a crucial role in SEO as they are an essential factor in determining the authority and relevance of a website. In simple terms, a backlink is a hyperlink from one website to another. Search engines, like Google, consider backlinks as a vote of confidence or endorsement for a website's content. The more high-quality and relevant backlinks a website has, the more likely it is to rank higher in search engine results.

Here are key points to understand the role of backlinks in SEO:

Authority and Trust: Backlinks act as indicators of a website's authority and trustworthiness. When reputable websites link to your content, it signals to search engines that your website provides valuable and credible information. Search engines view these endorsements as a positive signal and are more likely to rank your website higher in search results.

Improved Search Engine Rankings: Backlinks are an important ranking factor in search engine algorithms. Websites with a strong backlink profile tend to rank higher than those with fewer or low-quality backlinks. However, it's important to note that the quality and relevance of backlinks matter more than sheer quantity.

Referral Traffic: Backlinks not only impact your search engine rankings but also drive referral traffic to your website. When users click on a backlink from another website, they are directed to your site, potentially increasing your visibility and attracting new visitors. This can lead to more engagement, conversions, and growth for your online presence.

Natural and Organic Backlinks: Search engines value natural and organic backlinks more than manipulated or spammy ones. Natural backlinks are earned when other websites genuinely find your content valuable and link to it voluntarily. Focus on creating high-quality content that naturally attracts backlinks from authoritative sources within your niche.

Quality over Quantity: It's crucial to prioritize quality over quantity when it comes to backlinks. A few high-quality backlinks from reputable and relevant websites are more valuable than numerous low-quality backlinks. Aim to obtain backlinks from websites that have a strong reputation, high domain authority, and are relevant to your industry or topic.

Diversified Backlink Profile: Having a diverse backlink profile is important to demonstrate your website's authority and relevance across different sources. Seek backlinks from a variety of websites, including blogs, news sites, industry directories, and social media platforms. This diversity helps establish your website's credibility and improves its overall visibility.

Link Building Strategies: Implement effective link building strategies to acquire high-quality backlinks. This can include guest blogging, reaching out to influencers or industry experts, participating in online communities or forums, creating shareable content, and building relationships with other website owners or bloggers within your niche.

Monitor and Disavow Low-Quality Backlinks: Regularly monitor your backlink profile to ensure it remains clean and free from low-quality or spammy backlinks. If you identify any suspicious or harmful backlinks that may negatively impact your website's SEO, use the disavow tool provided by search engines to instruct them not to consider those links when evaluating your website.

Remember, backlinks should be obtained naturally and organically, indicating that your content is valuable and worthy of recognition. Focus on creating high-quality content, implementing effective link building strategies, and maintaining a healthy backlink profile to boost your website's authority, visibility, and overall SEO performance.

Strategies For Acquiring High-Quality Backlinks

Acquiring high-quality backlinks requires a strategic approach and a focus on building relationships and creating valuable content. Here are some effective strategies to help you acquire high-quality backlinks:

Create Outstanding Content: Develop high-quality, valuable, and shareable content that naturally attracts backlinks. This could be in the form of informative blog posts, in-depth guides, research studies, infographics, or interactive content. Content that provides unique insights, solves problems, or offers a fresh perspective is more likely to be linked to by other websites.

Guest Blogging: Contribute guest posts to reputable and relevant websites within your industry. Guest blogging allows you to showcase your expertise, reach a new audience, and gain valuable backlinks. When pitching guest posts, focus on providing valuable content that aligns with the host website's audience and guidelines.

Build Relationships: Connect and build relationships with influencers, bloggers, industry experts, and website owners in your niche. Engage with them through social media, comments on their blog posts, and attending industry events. Building relationships can lead to opportunities for collaboration, guest blogging, and natural backlinks as they become familiar with your work.

Broken Link Building: Find broken links on relevant websites and offer to replace them with your own relevant content. This approach helps website owners by fixing broken links, and in return, you gain a valuable backlink. Use tools like Check My Links or Broken Link Checker to identify broken links.

Resource Link Building: Create comprehensive resource pages or content hubs on your website that provide valuable information and resources related to your industry. Reach out to other website owners and let them know about your resource. If they find it valuable, they may link to it as a helpful reference for their audience.

Social Media Engagement: Actively engage on social media platforms related to your niche. Share your content, participate in relevant discussions, and build relationships with influencers and industry leaders. This can lead to natural backlinks as others discover and share your content.

Press Releases and Media Coverage: Utilize press releases and media outreach to gain exposure and potential backlinks from news outlets and industry publications. Ensure that your press releases are newsworthy and provide value to the readers. Journalists and bloggers may pick up your story and link back to your website.

Competitor Analysis: Analyze your competitors' backlink profiles to identify potential link building opportunities. Look for websites that are linking to your competitors but not to you. Reach out to those websites and offer them your valuable content or propose collaboration opportunities.

Participate in Online Communities and Forums: Engage in online communities and forums related to your industry. Provide helpful insights, answer questions, and share your expertise. As you establish yourself as a valuable contributor, others may link to your website as a trusted resource.

Influencer Outreach: Identify influencers within your industry and reach out to them for potential collaborations, interviews, or testimonials. If they find your content valuable, they may share it with their audience and provide you with a valuable backlink.

Remember, the key to acquiring high-quality backlinks is to focus on providing value, building relationships, and creating outstanding content. Always prioritize quality over quantity, and aim for natural and organic backlinks that reflect the credibility and relevance of your website.

Guest Blogging And Influencer Outreach

Guest blogging and influencer outreach are two effective strategies for acquiring high-quality backlinks. Let's explore each strategy in more detail:

Guest Blogging: Guest blogging involves writing and publishing articles on other websites within your industry or niche. It allows you to showcase your expertise, reach a new audience, and gain valuable backlinks. Here's how you can approach guest blogging effectively:

- Identify Relevant Websites: Look for websites that are relevant to your industry and have an audience that aligns with your target market. Make sure the websites have a good reputation and a decent level of traffic.
- Research Content Guidelines: Familiarize yourself with the guest blogging guidelines of the websites you want to contribute to. Pay attention to their preferred topics, word count, formatting, and any specific guidelines they may have.
- Craft High-Quality Content: Develop well-researched, informative, and engaging content that provides value to the readers. Focus on solving problems, sharing insights, or offering practical tips. Ensure that your content is unique and stands out from what's already available online.
- Outreach and Pitch: Contact the website owners or editors with a personalized email introducing yourself and your proposed guest post. Clearly explain the topic and outline of your article and highlight how it will benefit their audience. Tailor your pitch to show that you've done your research and understand their website's content.
- Follow Editorial Guidelines: Once your guest post is accepted, adhere to the website's editorial guidelines.

Craft the article based on their specifications, including any preferred writing style, tone, or formatting. Make sure to include a bio section with a link back to your own website.

- Promote Your Guest Post: Once your guest post is published, promote it on your own social media platforms and website. This helps to drive traffic to the host website and increases the visibility of your content.

Influencer Outreach: Influencer outreach involves connecting with influential individuals in your industry or niche to establish relationships and seek collaboration opportunities. Here's how you can approach influencer outreach effectively:

- Identify Relevant Influencers: Research and identify influencers who have a significant following and influence within your industry. Look for individuals who are active on social media, have popular blogs, or frequently appear as speakers or experts in your field.
- Engage and Build Relationships: Begin by engaging with the influencer's content on social media platforms, such as commenting, sharing, and tagging them. Show genuine interest in their work and contribute valuable insights to their discussions. Building a relationship takes time and requires consistent engagement.
- Provide Value: Offer value to the influencer by sharing relevant and insightful content, giving feedback on their work, or helping them with their projects. Look for opportunities to collaborate, such as co-creating content, participating in interviews, or hosting joint webinars.
- Personalized Outreach: When reaching out to influencers, craft personalized and genuine messages that highlight why you admire their work and how you believe a collaboration or endorsement could be mutually beneficial. Be specific about the value you can bring to their audience.

- Follow Up and Maintain Relationships: After the initial outreach, follow up to ensure your message was received. Stay connected with influencers by regularly engaging with their content and supporting their initiatives. Building long-term relationships with influencers can lead to ongoing collaborations and the potential for natural backlinks.

Remember, both guest blogging and influencer outreach require a thoughtful and genuine approach. Focus on building relationships, providing value, and creating meaningful collaborations. By doing so, you can acquire high-quality backlinks and expand your online visibility within your industry.

Social Media And Online Community Engagement

Social media and online community engagement play a crucial role in SEO by driving traffic to your website, increasing brand visibility, and fostering meaningful connections with your target audience. Here are some strategies to effectively engage on social media and online communities:

Choose the Right Platforms: Identify the social media platforms and online communities where your target audience is most active. Focus your efforts on platforms like Facebook, Twitter, Instagram, LinkedIn, or niche-specific forums and discussion boards.

Consistent Brand Presence: Maintain a consistent brand presence across your social media profiles. Use your brand logo, colors, and messaging to create a cohesive identity. Optimize your profiles by including relevant keywords in your bio and providing a link to your website.

Content Sharing: Share valuable and engaging content on social media platforms. Create a mix of content types, including blog articles, infographics, videos, and images. Optimize your content for each platform by understanding their specific requirements and best practices.

Engage with Your Audience: Actively engage with your audience by responding to comments, messages, and mentions. Encourage discussions, ask questions, and seek feedback to generate interactions. Show genuine interest in your audience's thoughts and opinions.

Hashtags and Keywords: Utilize relevant hashtags and keywords in your social media posts to increase visibility. Research popular and industry-specific hashtags and incorporate them strategically in your content. This helps your posts appear in relevant searches and discussions.

Online Community Participation: Join online communities and forums related to your niche. Contribute valuable insights, answer questions, and engage in discussions. Avoid overt self-promotion and focus on building credibility and trust within the community.

Influencer Collaboration: Collaborate with influencers or industry experts to amplify your reach. Partner with them for social media takeovers, co-create content, or participate in joint events. Their endorsement and promotion can significantly boost your visibility and credibility.

Social Sharing Buttons: Incorporate social sharing buttons on your website and blog posts to encourage readers to share your content on their social media profiles. Make it easy for visitors to engage with your content and spread the word.

Analyze and Adjust: Regularly monitor and analyze your social media and community engagement efforts. Track metrics like reach, engagement, and click-through rates. Identify what works best for your audience and adjust your strategies accordingly.

Remember, effective social media and online community engagement require authenticity, consistency, and value. Build relationships, provide meaningful interactions, and share valuable content to establish yourself as a trusted authority in your industry. By doing so, you can drive traffic to your website, improve your online visibility, and enhance your SEO efforts.

Measuring and Analyzing SEO Performance

Setting Up Google Analytics And Search Console

Setting up Google Analytics and Google Search Console is essential for monitoring and analyzing the performance of your website in search engines. Here's a step-by-step guide to setting up these tools:

Google Analytics:

- Sign in to your Google account or create a new one.
- Go to the Google Analytics website (https://analytics.google.com/) and click on "Start for free."
- Click on "Sign up" and provide the necessary information, including your website name, URL, industry category, and time zone.
- Select the data sharing options according to your preference.
- Read and accept the Google Analytics terms of service.
- You will be provided with a tracking ID and a tracking code snippet.
- Copy the tracking code snippet and paste it into the header section of your website's HTML code. This allows Google Analytics to collect data from your website.
- Save and publish the changes to your website.

Google Search Console:

- Sign in to your Google account or create a new one.

- Go to the Google Search Console website (https://search.google.com/search-console) and click on "Start now."
- Enter your website URL and click on "Continue."
- Verify ownership of your website by following the verification instructions provided by Google. This may involve adding a meta tag to your website's HTML code or uploading an HTML file to your website's root directory.
- Once verified, you will have access to the Google Search Console dashboard.
- Submit your sitemap to Google Search Console. This helps Google crawl and index your website more efficiently. You can generate a sitemap using various online tools or plugins available for your website's content management system.
- Monitor the performance of your website in Google Search Console. Explore the different sections and reports available, such as Search Analytics, Index Coverage, and URL Inspection, to gain insights into your website's visibility and search performance.

By setting up Google Analytics and Google Search Console, you gain valuable insights into your website's traffic, user behavior, search rankings, and indexing status. These tools provide you with data and metrics to optimize your website, make informed decisions, and improve your overall SEO strategy. Regularly review and analyze the data from these tools to identify areas for improvement and track the impact of your SEO efforts.

Tracking Keyword Rankings And Organic Traffic

Tracking keyword rankings and organic traffic is crucial for evaluating the effectiveness of your SEO strategies and monitoring the performance of your website. Here are some methods and tools to help you track keyword rankings and organic traffic:

Google Search Console: Google Search Console provides valuable insights into your website's organic search performance. It shows the keywords that are driving traffic to your site and their average position in search results. Use the Search Analytics report to track keyword rankings, impressions, clicks, and click-through rates (CTRs).

Rank Tracking Tools: There are several rank tracking tools available that allow you to monitor your keyword rankings across search engines. Some popular tools include SEMrush, Ahrefs, Moz, and Serpstat. These tools provide comprehensive data on keyword positions, search volumes, and historical trends.

Google Analytics: In addition to tracking overall website traffic, Google Analytics can help you monitor organic traffic specifically. Use the "Organic Search" segment in the Acquisition section to analyze the number of organic sessions, bounce rates, and other engagement metrics. You can also set up custom reports to track specific keywords or landing pages.

Manual Search: Perform manual searches on search engines using your target keywords to see where your website ranks. Make sure to log the results and track any changes over time. Keep in mind that search results can vary based on factors such as location, search history, and personalization, so it's useful to use incognito or private browsing mode.

Historical Data: Maintain a record of your keyword rankings and organic traffic over time. This allows you to identify trends, track progress, and evaluate the impact of your SEO efforts. Consider using spreadsheets or dedicated SEO tools to store and analyze historical data.

Competitor Analysis: Monitor the keyword rankings and organic traffic of your competitors. This helps you gain insights into their strategies, identify potential opportunities, and benchmark your performance against industry competitors. Tools like SEMrush and Ahrefs offer competitive analysis features for tracking competitor rankings and organic visibility.

Regularly track and analyze keyword rankings and organic traffic to understand how your website is performing in search engine results. Use the data to refine your SEO strategies, identify areas for improvement, and adapt your content and optimization efforts accordingly. Remember that SEO is an ongoing process, and tracking your progress is essential for continuous growth and success.

Analyzing User Behavior And Conversion Metrics

Analyzing user behavior and conversion metrics is crucial for understanding how visitors interact with your website and optimizing it for better conversions. Here are some strategies and tools to help you analyze user behavior and conversion metrics:

Google Analytics: Google Analytics provides valuable insights into user behavior on your website. It offers metrics such as bounce rate, average session duration, pages per session, and goal completions. Utilize the Behavior Flow report to visualize the user journey on your site and identify areas where visitors drop off or engage the most.

Heatmaps and Click Tracking: Heatmap tools like Hotjar and Crazy Egg allow you to visually analyze user behavior by displaying where visitors click, scroll, and spend the most time on your web pages. These insights can help you identify popular content, areas of interest, and potential usability issues.

Conversion Funnels: Set up conversion funnels in Google Analytics to track the steps users take to complete specific goals on your website, such as signing up for a newsletter or making a purchase. Analyzing the funnel helps you identify bottlenecks and areas where users drop off, allowing you to optimize those stages for higher conversion rates.

A/B Testing: Conduct A/B tests to compare different versions of your web pages and measure the impact on conversion rates. Tools like Optimizely and Google Optimize allow you to test variations of headlines, calls-to-action, layouts, and other elements to determine which version performs better.

Exit Surveys and Feedback: Implement exit surveys or feedback forms on your website to gather insights directly from visitors. This can provide valuable qualitative data on their experience, pain points, and suggestions for improvement.

E-commerce Tracking: If you run an e-commerce website, enable e-commerce tracking in Google Analytics to analyze purchase behavior, product performance, and revenue. This data can help you optimize your product offerings, pricing, and checkout process.

User Testing: Conduct user testing sessions where individuals from your target audience navigate and interact with your website while providing feedback. User testing can reveal usability issues, confusion points, and opportunities for enhancing the user experience.

By analyzing user behavior and conversion metrics, you can gain insights into how visitors engage with your website, identify areas for improvement, and optimize your site to increase conversions. Regularly monitor these metrics and make data-driven decisions to enhance user experience and achieve your conversion goals.

Utilizing Seo Reporting And Data-Driven Decision Making

Utilizing SEO reporting and data-driven decision making is essential for optimizing your SEO strategy and achieving better results. Here's how you can make the most of SEO reporting and data to drive your decisions:

Track Key Performance Indicators (KPIs): Identify and track relevant KPIs to measure the success of your SEO efforts. These may include organic traffic, keyword rankings, backlink profile, conversion rates, and bounce rate. Regularly monitor these metrics to assess your progress and identify areas for improvement.

Set Up Customized SEO Reports: Utilize tools like Google Analytics, Google Search Console, and SEO platforms to generate customized reports that provide insights into your website's performance. These reports can help you understand keyword rankings, organic traffic sources, user behavior, and other crucial SEO metrics.

Analyze Keyword Data: Review keyword data to identify which keywords are driving the most traffic and conversions. Look for opportunities to optimize existing content or create new content targeting high-potential keywords with significant search volume and low competition.

Conduct Competitor Analysis: Analyze your competitors' SEO strategies and performance. Identify keywords they are targeting, backlinks they have acquired, and content they are producing. This information can help you identify gaps and areas where you can outperform them.

Identify Technical SEO Issues: Use SEO auditing tools to scan your website for technical issues that may affect its performance and search visibility. Look for issues like broken links, duplicate content, slow page load speed, and mobile-friendliness. Address these issues promptly to improve your website's SEO health.

Monitor Backlink Profile: Regularly monitor your backlink profile to ensure the quality and relevance of the sites linking to your website. Identify and disavow any toxic or spammy backlinks that can harm your SEO efforts.

Utilize A/B Testing: Conduct A/B tests to compare different SEO strategies or website elements. Test variations of meta titles, descriptions, content formats, and page layouts to determine which version performs better. Use the data from these tests to refine your SEO approach.

Make Data-Driven Decisions: Base your SEO decisions on data and insights rather than assumptions or guesswork. Use the information from your SEO reports and analysis to make informed decisions about keyword targeting, content optimization, website improvements, and overall SEO strategy.

Continuously Adapt and Evolve: SEO is an ongoing process, and the digital landscape is constantly evolving. Regularly review your SEO reports, monitor industry trends, and stay updated with algorithm changes to adapt your strategy accordingly.

By utilizing SEO reporting and data-driven decision making, you can effectively measure the performance of your SEO efforts, identify areas for improvement, and make informed decisions to enhance your website's search visibility and drive organic traffic.

Advanced SEO Techniques and Trends

Voice Search Optimization

Voice search optimization has become increasingly important as more people use voice assistants and smart speakers to search for information. Here are some strategies to optimize your website for voice search:

Understand Natural Language: Voice search queries tend to be more conversational and longer than traditional typed searches. Optimize your content to match the natural language patterns that users employ when speaking their queries. Consider incorporating long-tail keywords and phrases that reflect how people would ask a question verbally.

Featured Snippets: Featured snippets, also known as "Position Zero" results, are the concise answers that appear at the top of search results. These snippets are highly coveted in voice search as voice assistants often read out the featured snippet as the answer to a query. Structure your content in a way that provides clear and concise answers to commonly asked questions related to your topic to increase the chances of being featured.

Page Speed Optimization: Voice search users often expect fast and immediate results. Ensure that your website loads quickly on both desktop and mobile devices. Optimize images, minify code, and leverage caching techniques to improve page speed. Consider implementing Accelerated Mobile Pages (AMP) to provide faster loading times for mobile users.

Local SEO Optimization: Many voice searches are location-specific, such as "find restaurants near me" or "what's the closest coffee shop?" Optimize your website and Google My Business listing for local SEO by including relevant local keywords, updating your address and contact information, and encouraging online reviews.

Schema Markup: Implement structured data markup on your website to provide search engines with specific information about your content. This helps search engines better understand and interpret your content, increasing the chances of being featured in voice search results. Use schema markup to highlight key information such as business hours, product details, event information, and more.

Conversational Tone and Natural Language: When creating content, write in a conversational tone that mimics how people speak. Use natural language and avoid overly technical jargon or complex sentences. This makes your content more accessible and aligns with the way users formulate voice search queries.

Mobile-Friendly Design: Voice searches are often conducted on mobile devices. Ensure that your website is mobile-friendly, with responsive design and a user-friendly interface. Optimize your website for smaller screens and ensure that buttons and links are easy to tap and navigate.

Local Business Listings and Directories: Ensure that your business information is accurate and up-to-date on various local business directories, such as Google My Business, Yelp, and Bing Places. This improves the likelihood of your business being recommended in voice searches related to your industry and location.

Natural Language FAQs: Create a Frequently Asked Questions (FAQ) page that addresses common queries in a natural language format. Consider the types of questions users might ask in voice search and provide clear and concise answers.

By implementing these voice search optimization strategies, you can improve your website's visibility and relevance in voice search results, reaching a broader audience and capturing valuable organic traffic from voice-enabled devices.

Local Seo Strategies For Businesses

Local SEO strategies play a crucial role in helping businesses improve their online visibility and attract local customers. Here are some effective local SEO strategies:

Google My Business (GMB) Optimization: Create and optimize your Google My Business listing, ensuring that all the information is accurate and up-to-date. Include your business name, address, phone number (NAP), website URL, business hours, and relevant categories. Encourage customers to leave reviews, respond to reviews promptly, and upload photos that showcase your business.

Local Keyword Optimization: Conduct keyword research to identify relevant local keywords for your business. Incorporate these keywords naturally into your website content, meta tags, headings, and image alt tags. Focus on location-based keywords to target customers in your area.

Online Directories and Citations: Ensure your business information is consistent across online directories, such as Yelp, Yellow Pages, and industry-specific directories. Include your NAP details, website URL, and a brief description of your business. This helps search engines verify your business information and improves your local search rankings.

Location-Specific Landing Pages: Create dedicated landing pages on your website for each location or service area you serve. Optimize these pages with relevant local keywords and provide detailed information about your products, services, and contact details specific to each location.

Online Reviews and Ratings: Encourage customers to leave reviews on platforms like Google My Business, Yelp, and other review sites. Positive reviews help build credibility and improve your local search rankings. Respond to reviews, both positive and negative, to show that you value customer feedback.

Local Citations and Backlinks: Earn local citations and backlinks from reputable local websites and directories. This helps search engines understand the relevance and authority of your business in the local area. Participate in local events, sponsor local organizations, and seek partnerships to increase your chances of earning local citations and backlinks.

Location-Specific Content: Create content that caters to local audiences. Write blog posts, articles, or guides that focus on local topics, events, or news. This helps establish your expertise in the local community and attracts local customers.

Mobile-Friendly and Responsive Design: Optimize your website for mobile devices as many local searches are conducted on smartphones. Ensure your website has a responsive design, loads quickly, and provides a seamless user experience across all devices.

Local Schema Markup: Implement local schema markup on your website to provide search engines with detailed information about your business, such as address, phone number, business hours, and customer reviews. This helps search engines understand your business and display relevant information in search results.

Local Business Listings: Create and optimize listings on local business directories and review sites specific to your industry and location. This includes platforms like TripAdvisor, Angie's List, and industry-specific directories. Include accurate and consistent business information, along with compelling descriptions and images.

Social Media Localization: Leverage social media platforms to engage with the local community. Share local events, news, and customer stories. Encourage user-generated content by running contests or featuring customers' posts. Engage with local influencers and collaborate on content or promotions to expand your reach.

Geotargeted Advertising: Utilize geotargeted advertising to reach local customers. Platforms like Google Ads and social media advertising allow you to target specific locations with your ads, ensuring that your message reaches the right audience.

Local Link Building: Build relationships with other local businesses, organizations, and influencers to earn local backlinks. Collaborate on content, sponsor local events, or contribute guest posts to local blogs. These partnerships can help boost your local SEO efforts.

Monitor and Respond to Local Search Results: Regularly monitor your local search rankings and adjust your strategy accordingly. Pay attention to the local pack results and featured snippets in your target area. Optimize your content and website based on the performance of specific local search queries.

By implementing these local SEO strategies, businesses can improve their visibility in local search results and attract customers from their target areas. Remember, consistency, relevance, and engagement with the local community are key factors in successful local SEO.

Schema Markup And Rich Snippets

Schema markup and rich snippets play a crucial role in enhancing the visibility and click-through rates of your website in search engine results. By incorporating structured data markup into your website's HTML code, you provide search engines with additional information about your content, helping them understand and present it more effectively to users.

What is Schema Markup: Schema markup is a standardized vocabulary of tags or microdata that you add to your HTML code. It provides context and additional details about the content on your website, such as product information, reviews, events, recipes, and more.

Benefits of Schema Markup: Implementing schema markup offers several benefits, including:

- Improved Search Results: Schema markup helps search engines create rich snippets, which are enhanced search results that display additional information about your web page, such as ratings, prices, and descriptions. Rich snippets attract attention and increase click-through rates.
- Enhanced Visibility: Schema markup helps search engines understand the context of your content, allowing them to display it in relevant search results. This improves your website's visibility to users searching for specific information or topics.
- Better User Experience: Rich snippets provide users with valuable information upfront, allowing them to make informed decisions without clicking through to your website. This improves the user experience and increases the chances of attracting qualified traffic.

Common Schema Markup Types: There are various schema markup types available for different content types, including:

- Product: Markup for products, including details like name, price, availability, and reviews.
- Recipe: Markup for recipes, including ingredients, cooking time, and nutrition information.
- Local Business: Markup for local businesses, providing details like address, phone number, and operating hours.
- Event: Markup for events, including date, time, location, and ticket information.
- Article: Markup for news articles, blog posts, and other written content, including headline, author, and publishing date.

Implementing Schema Markup: You can implement schema markup by adding structured data to your HTML code manually or using a plugin or tool that generates the markup for you. Google's Structured Data Markup Helper and Schema.org are useful resources for generating and validating schema markup.

Testing and Monitoring: After implementing schema markup, it's crucial to test and monitor its performance. Use Google's Structured Data Testing Tool to ensure that the markup is implemented correctly and that search engines can understand and interpret it. Additionally, regularly monitor your search engine rankings and appearance in search results to assess the impact of schema markup on your website's visibility.

By leveraging schema markup and rich snippets, you can enhance your website's visibility, attract more targeted traffic, and provide users with valuable information right in the search results. Implementing schema markup requires technical expertise, but the benefits in terms of increased visibility and improved click-through rates make it a worthwhile investment for your SEO strategy.

Seo For E-Commerce Websites

SEO for e-commerce websites is crucial for driving organic traffic, improving search engine rankings, and ultimately increasing sales. Implementing effective SEO strategies can help your e-commerce website stand out in a competitive online marketplace. Here are some key considerations for optimizing your e-commerce site:

Keyword Research: Conduct thorough keyword research to identify the relevant keywords and phrases that your target audience is using to search for products. Focus on long-tail keywords that have high search volume and lower competition. Incorporate these keywords naturally into your product descriptions, titles, headings, and URLs.

On-Page Optimization: Optimize each product page individually by including unique and descriptive titles and meta descriptions. Ensure that your product descriptions are well-written, informative, and include relevant keywords. Optimize your product images by using descriptive file names and alt tags.

Site Structure and Navigation: Ensure that your website has a clear and intuitive structure that allows users to easily navigate through your product categories and pages. Implement a logical hierarchy of categories and subcategories, and use breadcrumbs for easy navigation. Make sure that your website is mobile-friendly, as mobile usage continues to rise.

User Reviews and Ratings: Encourage customers to leave reviews and ratings for your products. User-generated content adds credibility to your products and can improve search engine rankings. Implement a review system and make it easy for customers to leave feedback.

Technical SEO: Pay attention to technical aspects such as website speed, mobile responsiveness, and URL structure. Optimize your site for fast loading times, as slow websites can negatively impact user experience and search engine rankings. Use canonical tags to avoid duplicate content issues.

Link Building: Build high-quality backlinks to your e-commerce site through content marketing, guest blogging, influencer collaborations, and partnerships. Seek opportunities to have your products featured on relevant websites or blogs, and participate in industry-specific forums or communities to establish your brand's authority.

Optimized Product Images: Optimize your product images by using descriptive file names, compressing them for faster loading, and adding alt tags that include relevant keywords. Optimized images improve user experience, increase the chances of appearing in image search results, and contribute to overall SEO efforts.

Implement Structured Data Markup: Use schema markup to provide search engines with additional information about your products, such as price, availability, ratings, and reviews. This can enhance your appearance in search results and attract more qualified traffic.

Content Marketing: Develop a content marketing strategy that includes creating informative and engaging content related to your products. Publish blog posts, guides, tutorials, and product comparisons to attract organic traffic and establish your brand as an authority in your industry.

Monitor and Analyze: Regularly monitor your website's performance using tools like Google Analytics and Google Search Console. Analyze data such as traffic sources, user behavior, conversion rates, and keyword rankings. Use this data to identify areas for improvement and refine your SEO strategy.

Remember that SEO for e-commerce is an ongoing process. Stay up to date with the latest industry trends and search engine algorithm updates, and continuously optimize your website for better visibility, higher rankings, and increased conversions.

SEO Best Practices and Future Considerations

Staying Updated With Search Engine Algorithm Changes

Staying updated with search engine algorithm changes is essential for maintaining a strong SEO strategy. Search engines like Google frequently update their algorithms to deliver the most relevant and high-quality search results to users. Here are some tips to help you stay informed about algorithm changes:

Follow Official Channels: Stay connected with official channels such as Google Webmaster Central Blog, Bing Webmaster Blog, and other search engine blogs. These blogs often announce major algorithm updates, provide insights, and offer recommendations to improve your website's performance.

Industry Publications and Websites: Keep an eye on industry publications, news websites, and blogs that cover SEO and search engine updates. Websites like Search Engine Land, Moz, Search Engine Journal, and SEMrush often provide in-depth analysis and news about algorithm changes.

Webmaster Forums and Communities: Engage in webmaster forums and online communities where SEO professionals and website owners share insights and discuss algorithm changes. Platforms like Reddit's SEO community and forums like WebmasterWorld and Black Hat World can be valuable sources of information.

Google Search Console: Regularly monitor your website's performance in Google Search Console. It provides valuable data about your website's visibility, indexing, and search traffic. Look for any notifications or messages from Google that may highlight algorithm changes or issues affecting your website.

Webinars and Conferences: Attend webinars and conferences that focus on SEO and digital marketing. Industry experts and speakers often share the latest trends, algorithm updates, and best practices. These events provide valuable insights and networking opportunities.

SEO Tools and Software: Utilize SEO tools and software that offer algorithm monitoring and update notifications. Tools like Moz, SEMrush, Ahrefs, and Rank Ranger provide alerts and tracking features to keep you informed about algorithm changes and their impact on your website's performance.

Follow SEO Experts and Influencers: Follow reputable SEO experts and influencers on social media platforms, such as Twitter and LinkedIn. They often share valuable insights, analysis, and updates about search engine algorithms.

Experiment and Monitor: Continuously experiment with different SEO techniques and monitor their impact on your website's performance. Keep track of any significant changes in search rankings, organic traffic, and user engagement metrics. This way, you can identify potential algorithmic shifts and adjust your strategy accordingly.

Remember that algorithm updates can have both positive and negative impacts on your website's rankings. Focus on building a strong foundation of SEO best practices, such as creating high-quality content, optimizing your website's technical aspects, and providing a great user experience. By staying updated and adapting your SEO strategy, you can maintain and improve your website's visibility in search engine results pages.

Building Long-Term, Sustainable Seo Strategies

Building long-term, sustainable SEO strategies is crucial for consistent and lasting success in search engine optimization. Here are some key principles to consider when developing your strategy:

Focus on User Experience: Put the user at the center of your SEO efforts. Create valuable and engaging content that meets the needs and expectations of your target audience. Ensure your website is user-friendly, intuitive to navigate, and optimized for different devices. By prioritizing user experience, you'll naturally align with search engine algorithms that aim to deliver the best user experience.

Conduct Comprehensive Keyword Research: Thorough keyword research is essential for understanding the language and intent of your target audience. Identify relevant keywords and phrases that align with your business and optimize your content around them. Aim for a balance between high search volume and low competition keywords to maximize your chances of ranking well.

Create High-Quality Content: Develop a content strategy that focuses on producing high-quality, valuable, and unique content. Craft content that addresses the needs, questions, and interests of your target audience. Use a variety of content formats, such as articles, videos, infographics, and podcasts, to cater to different preferences and enhance engagement.

Optimize On-Page Elements: Pay attention to on-page optimization factors, including title tags, meta descriptions, headers, and URL structure. Incorporate relevant keywords naturally into your content without overstuffing. Ensure your pages load quickly, are mobile-friendly, and have descriptive and compelling meta information that encourages click-throughs from search engine results.

Build High-Quality Backlinks: Earn authoritative and relevant backlinks from reputable websites in your industry. Focus on natural link building through valuable content, outreach to influencers and industry experts, and participating in relevant online communities. Quality backlinks signal to search engines that your website is trusted and authoritative.

Leverage Social Media and Content Promotion: Utilize social media platforms to amplify your content and reach a wider audience. Share your content across relevant social channels, engage with your audience, and encourage social sharing. Actively promote your content through email marketing, influencer collaborations, and partnerships to increase visibility and attract organic backlinks.

Monitor, Analyze, and Adapt: Regularly monitor your website's performance using web analytics tools such as Google Analytics. Track important metrics like organic traffic, conversion rates, bounce rates, and keyword rankings. Analyze the data to identify trends, patterns, and areas for improvement. Adjust your SEO strategies based on data insights and market changes to stay competitive.

Stay Informed and Evolve: SEO is a dynamic field that continually evolves. Stay up to date with industry trends, algorithm updates, and best practices. Follow reputable SEO resources, participate in industry forums and communities, and attend relevant conferences and webinars. Embrace a mindset of continuous learning and adaptation to keep your SEO strategies effective.

Remember, building a sustainable SEO strategy takes time and dedication. It's a long-term investment that requires consistent effort, optimization, and adaptation. By focusing on user experience, creating high-quality content, and staying informed about SEO best practices, you can establish a strong foundation for long-term success in driving organic traffic and improving search engine rankings.

Addressing Common Seo Challenges And Mistakes

Addressing common SEO challenges and avoiding mistakes is crucial for achieving optimal results in your SEO efforts. Here are some common challenges and mistakes to be aware of, along with strategies to overcome them:

Lack of Keyword Research: Failing to conduct thorough keyword research can hinder your SEO success. Ensure you identify relevant keywords and phrases that align with your target audience's search intent. Use keyword research tools to discover high-volume, low-competition keywords, and incorporate them strategically into your content.

Poor Website Structure: A poorly structured website can impede search engine crawlers from properly indexing and understanding your content. Ensure your website has a clear and intuitive hierarchy, with organized categories, subcategories, and internal linking. Optimize your URL structure to be descriptive and user-friendly.

Thin or Low-Quality Content: Content is a critical component of SEO. Thin or low-quality content that lacks depth, relevance, or value will not rank well in search results. Focus on creating comprehensive, informative, and engaging content that satisfies user intent and provides unique insights or solutions.

Neglecting On-Page Optimization: On-page optimization elements, such as title tags, meta descriptions, headers, and keyword placement, play a significant role in SEO. Neglecting these elements can result in missed opportunities for search engine visibility. Ensure you optimize each page with relevant keywords and compelling meta information to improve click-through rates.

Ignoring Mobile Optimization: With the increasing use of mobile devices, optimizing your website for mobile is crucial. Neglecting mobile optimization can lead to poor user experience and lower search engine rankings. Make your website responsive, ensure fast page loading times, and provide a seamless mobile browsing experience.

Neglecting Link Building: Building high-quality backlinks is essential for improving your website's authority and search engine rankings. Neglecting link building can limit your organic traffic potential. Implement a link-building strategy that focuses on acquiring relevant and authoritative backlinks from reputable sources through outreach, content promotion, and guest blogging.

Overlooking Technical SEO Issues: Technical SEO encompasses various aspects, such as website speed, crawlability, indexability, and schema markup. Ignoring technical SEO issues can hinder your website's performance in search engine rankings. Regularly conduct technical audits to identify and resolve any issues that may negatively impact your SEO efforts.

Lack of Regular Monitoring and Analysis: SEO requires continuous monitoring and analysis to identify areas for improvement. Failing to track key metrics, analyze data, and adapt your strategies can hinder your progress. Utilize analytics tools to monitor organic traffic, keyword rankings, user behavior, and conversion rates. Use the insights to make data-driven decisions and optimize your SEO campaigns.

By addressing these common challenges and avoiding mistakes, you can enhance the effectiveness of your SEO efforts. Stay proactive, stay informed about industry updates, and be willing to adapt your strategies as needed. SEO is an ongoing process, and by continuously refining your approach, you can achieve better search engine visibility, increased organic traffic, and improved online visibility.

Embracing Emerging Seo Trends And Technologies

Embracing emerging SEO trends and technologies is crucial for staying ahead of the competition and maximizing your SEO efforts. Here are some key trends and technologies to consider:

Voice Search Optimization: With the rise of voice assistants like Siri, Alexa, and Google Assistant, optimizing your content for voice search has become essential. Voice search queries tend to be more conversational, so incorporating long-tail keywords and natural language into your content can help improve your visibility in voice search results.

Mobile-First Indexing: As mobile usage continues to dominate, search engines have shifted towards mobile-first indexing. This means that search engines prioritize the mobile version of websites when determining rankings. Ensure your website is mobile-friendly, responsive, and provides a seamless user experience across different devices.

Artificial Intelligence (AI) and Machine Learning: AI and machine learning are revolutionizing SEO by enabling search engines to better understand user intent and deliver more relevant search results. Utilize AI-powered tools for keyword research, content optimization, and data analysis to gain insights and improve your SEO strategies.

Featured Snippets and Rich Results: Featured snippets are concise, direct answers displayed at the top of search results. Optimizing your content to appear in featured snippets can significantly increase your visibility and click-through rates. Implement structured data markup to enhance your chances of appearing in rich results like recipe cards, reviews, and product information.

User Experience (UX) Optimization: User experience has a significant impact on SEO. Search engines prioritize websites that provide a positive user experience. Focus on improving website speed, navigation, readability, and overall usability. Ensure your website is easy to navigate, loads quickly, and delivers high-quality content that meets user needs.

Video and Visual Content Optimization: Video content continues to gain popularity, and search engines increasingly prioritize video results in search rankings. Incorporate video content into your SEO strategy by optimizing video titles, descriptions, and tags. Create engaging and shareable visual content, such as infographics and images, to enhance user experience and increase engagement.

Local SEO: Local search optimization is crucial for businesses targeting a specific geographic area. Optimize your website and online listings for local keywords, claim your business on Google My Business, and encourage customer reviews. Utilize local directories and ensure your contact information is consistent across platforms.

Mobile-First Indexing: With the majority of online searches now happening on mobile devices, search engines prioritize mobile-friendly websites. Ensure your website is responsive, loads quickly, and provides a seamless user experience on mobile devices.

By embracing these emerging SEO trends and technologies, you can stay at the forefront of SEO best practices and leverage new opportunities for improving your online visibility and driving organic traffic. Stay informed about industry updates, experiment with new strategies, and adapt your approach to align with the evolving search landscape.

Conclusion

Recap Of Key Takeaways From The Guide

Throughout this guide, we have covered a wide range of topics related to SEO. Here's a recap of the key takeaways:

SEO is crucial in the digital age: It helps improve your online visibility, drive organic traffic, and increase your website's ranking in search engine results.

Understanding how search engines work: Search engines use complex algorithms to crawl and index web pages, considering factors like relevance, authority, and user experience to determine rankings.

Keywords are essential: Keywords play a vital role in SEO by helping search engines understand the relevance of your content. Conduct thorough keyword research and incorporate relevant keywords strategically throughout your website.

User experience matters: Providing a positive user experience is crucial for both search engines and website visitors. Ensure your website is user-friendly, mobile-responsive, and loads quickly.

High-quality content is key: Creating valuable, informative, and engaging content is essential for SEO success. Focus on producing high-quality content that satisfies user intent and incorporates relevant keywords.

Backlinks influence rankings: Building high-quality backlinks from authoritative websites signals to search engines that your content is trustworthy and valuable. Implement strategies to acquire quality backlinks.

Analytics and data-driven decisions: Utilize tools like Google Analytics and Search Console to track and analyze your website's performance, keyword rankings, and user behavior. Use this data to make informed decisions and optimize your SEO strategies.

Stay updated with algorithm changes: Search engine algorithms evolve constantly. Stay informed about algorithm updates and industry trends to adapt your SEO strategies accordingly.

Local SEO is essential for businesses: If you have a local business, optimize your online presence for local searches. Claim your Google My Business listing, encourage customer reviews, and ensure consistent NAP (name, address, phone number) information across platforms.

Embrace emerging trends and technologies: Stay ahead of the curve by incorporating emerging SEO trends and technologies into your strategies, such as voice search optimization, mobile-first indexing, AI-driven tools, and visual content optimization.

By implementing these key takeaways, you can enhance your website's visibility, attract more organic traffic, and improve your overall online presence. Remember that SEO is an ongoing process, and continuous optimization and adaptation are essential for long-term success.

Encouragement To Continue Mastering Seo

Congratulations on completing this comprehensive guide to mastering SEO! By delving into the intricacies of search engine optimization, you've acquired a valuable set of skills and knowledge that can propel your online success.

However, it's important to remember that SEO is a continuously evolving field. Search engine algorithms and user behaviors change over time, which means you need to stay up-to-date and continue honing your SEO skills. Embrace the mindset of continuous learning and improvement.

As you continue your SEO journey, here are a few words of encouragement:

Stay curious: SEO is a dynamic field, and there is always something new to discover. Stay curious and explore emerging trends, technologies, and strategies. Engage in industry forums, read SEO blogs, and attend conferences to stay abreast of the latest developments.

Experiment and test: SEO is not a one-size-fits-all approach. Every website and target audience is unique, so it's essential to experiment with different tactics and test their effectiveness. Use analytics tools to measure the impact of your SEO efforts and refine your strategies accordingly.

Embrace data-driven decision-making: Let data guide your SEO strategies. Regularly analyze your website's performance, keyword rankings, and user behavior to identify areas for improvement and make informed decisions. Utilize tools like Google Analytics and Search Console to gain valuable insights.

Network and collaborate: Surround yourself with fellow SEO enthusiasts and professionals. Engage in discussions, share insights, and learn from others' experiences. Collaborate with like-minded individuals on projects or case studies to expand your knowledge and perspective.

Celebrate your successes: Acknowledge and celebrate your achievements along the way. SEO can be a challenging journey, but remember to celebrate the milestones you reach and the progress you make. Each step forward brings you closer to achieving your goals.

Remember, mastering SEO is a continuous process. The digital landscape is ever-changing, and it's essential to adapt and evolve with it. By staying committed, remaining curious, and embracing the challenges and opportunities that arise, you can continue to refine your SEO skills and achieve even greater success in driving organic traffic, improving online visibility, and reaching your target audience. Keep up the great work, and happy optimizing!

Final Thoughts And Resources For Further Learning

In closing, I want to applaud your dedication to mastering SEO. By completing this comprehensive guide, you've gained a solid foundation of SEO knowledge and practical strategies. But the learning doesn't have to stop here. SEO is a vast and ever-evolving field, and there are always new techniques and insights to explore.

To continue your SEO journey and deepen your understanding, here are some resources and avenues for further learning:

Online SEO communities and forums: Engage with SEO professionals and enthusiasts in online communities such as Moz Community, Warrior Forum, or Reddit's SEO subreddit. Participate in discussions, ask questions, and learn from the experiences of others.

SEO blogs and publications: Follow reputable SEO blogs and publications like Moz, Search Engine Journal, Search Engine Land, Neil Patel, Backlinko, and Ahrefs. These platforms provide valuable insights, case studies, and the latest updates in the SEO industry.

Online courses and certifications: Consider enrolling in online SEO courses offered by platforms like Udemy, Coursera, and HubSpot Academy. These courses cover a wide range of SEO topics and provide structured learning paths to help you deepen your expertise.

Webinars and conferences: Attend webinars and industry conferences to stay updated on the latest trends and developments in SEO. Events like MozCon, Search Marketing Expo (SMX), and Pubcon bring together industry experts who share their knowledge and insights.

Experimentation and hands-on experience: Implement what you've learned by working on real SEO projects. Whether it's optimizing your own website, volunteering to help friends or small businesses with their SEO, or joining SEO-focused projects, hands-on experience is invaluable for honing your skills.

Stay updated with algorithm changes: Search engine algorithms evolve constantly, so staying informed about algorithm updates is crucial. Follow search engine news and official announcements to understand how these changes can impact your SEO strategies.

Remember, SEO is a long-term investment, and results may take time. Be patient, persistent, and open to adapting your strategies based on data and insights. Continually evaluate your efforts, measure performance, and refine your tactics to achieve sustainable growth.

Finally, I want to express my gratitude for choosing this guide and investing your time and effort in mastering SEO. The knowledge and skills you've gained will undoubtedly benefit your online endeavors. Best of luck on your SEO journey, and may your websites and content thrive in the search engine landscape!

www.ingramcontent.com/pod-product-compliance
Lightning Source LLC
LaVergne TN
LVHW051539050326
832903LV00033B/4337